COME TO JESUS

WHAT IF GOD DESIGNS YOUR DAYS
TO KEEP YOU RUNNING BACK TO HIM?

CHRISTA THRELFALL

Cover Design: Christa Threlfall
Author Photo: Courtney Taylor Bowles

First printing 2019 Printed in the United States of America Unless otherwise noted, Scripture quotations are from the ESV® Bible (The Holy Bible, English Standard Version®), copyright © 2001 by Crossway, a publishing ministry of Good News Publishers. Used by permission. All rights reserved.

ISBN: 9781790352517

Endorsements

"We need constant reminders that, in everything, we can go to Jesus. I'm grateful for Christa's helpful and beautiful call to do just that through the pages of this book."

- **Christine Hoover**, author of *Searching for Spring* and *Messy Beautiful Friendship*

"At this point in history, things look bleak for so many. And at this point in history, there are so many voices telling us how to fix our lives so that things will not look so bleak. Never before have we needed wise women to say it over and over again: Come to Jesus. He is the author. Come to Jesus, He is the fixer. Come to Jesus, He is the comfort. You'll love this gentle and timely word from Christa and it will leave you wanting more of Jesus, and knowing exactly where to find Him."

- **Jess Connolly**, coauthor of *Wild and Free* and author of *Dance Stand Run*

"Are you lonely? Overwhelmed? Battling unbelief? In this book, Christa speaks to women of all ages in a refreshingly simple yet profound style. She offers a glimpse into her own life to communicate the convincing message that you can and should come to Jesus regardless of who you are or where you find yourself in life."

- **Gretchen Fant**, speaker, counselor, and veteran pastor's wife

"This is the best kind of book: it accurately speaks God's truth, it illustrates how his truth has affected someone's life, and it gives us practical steps to apply truth to our own lives.

By candidly telling us how she has learned to run to Jesus, Christa has opened her heart to us in a way that every woman can relate to. In different places and different circumstances, we've all been where she is, wanting to walk in a God-pleasing way but stumbling over obstacles along the way. We need to help each other. Christa has allowed us to learn from her life by sharing her story of failures that have led to learning that has led to victory.

This small book has rooted itself in my heart, and since reading it, I've stopped in my wrong-way track more than once to remind myself to "run to Jesus" with my fears, doubts, sorrows, and temptations.

I'm grateful for how it is helping me. Like all good books, it's simple but profound, memorable, and full of truth."

- **Claudia Barba**, author of *Sovereign Hope*, *Refresh Your Heart*, and *The Monday Morning Club*

Dedication

To the One who had this idea in the first place,
prodded me to keep at it until it was completed,
and gave me strength to finish.

Thank you, Jesus, for teaching me that life works best
when I come to you rather than run from you.
You are better than I deserve.

Contents

Acknowledgments

There's always a story behind every book. It's the story of how the book came to be and who encouraged the author as she wrote.

There are many people who have encouraged me over the last seven years of my writing journey, but here are some who are specific to this book:

My parents and siblings: For being the first ones to read my book and encouraging me to publish it after reading it. Dad and Mom, you gave each of your kids a priceless gift as we grew up watching you bring your struggles to Jesus. I wouldn't be who I am today if it weren't for your loving, prayerful support. Mom, thanks for encouraging me in my writing journey ever since those horrible compositions I wrote during my homeschooling days. (Whew.) Becky, Sarah, and Josh—you are a constant encouragement to me as I watch your love for God and obedience to his Word. All of you are a gracious gift from God to me.

Brian and Christa: For being the first ones I actually voiced this idea to, asking thoughtful follow-up questions and encouraging me to think specifically about my writing goal. And for the tacos.

My blog readers: For your support, prayers, and kindness over the past years of my writing journey. God used you to put this seed of a book idea in my heart and I think it's completely accurate to say this book wouldn't be here if it weren't for you.

My dear Jonathan: For listening to me cry over this book and its message. For saying "You need to write this book" when I desperately wanted to quit. For being the first one to read it in all of its ugly "first draft-ness." For offering feedback and editing. For taking care of our kiddos and sending me away to write and pray. For being my best friend. You are the real MVP and I love you dearly.

Why I Wrote This Book

Why did I spend time writing this book when I could have used my time to actually tackle the laundry instead of finding creative places to stash piles of clean clothes? *(Putting them back in the dryer is a great idea for anyone wondering. As is the bathtub.)*

I want you to discover, along with me, what it means to come to Jesus with everything. "Everything" as in every little, tiny, seemingly insignificant thing. From the unkind comment made by the stranger at the grocery store to the life-shifting, world-rocking phone call.

I often learn best from reading stories, so I'm going to share a few with you. In this book, I'll walk you through the past few years of my life and the different situations in which God has taught me to come to him with everything. My goal in this storytelling is to put some flesh and blood on the idea of what it means to come to Jesus...not just saying, "Do it! Be blessed!" But rather, "Here's what God

1

brought in my life. This is how I fought him. And this is how God gave peace when I surrendered and came back to him."

What would your relationship with God look like if you took every difficulty in your day today and brought it to his feet? "God, I can't handle this. You're going to have to take this one for me."

I wrote this book because I want you to find out.

The Lesson

There are some memories so painful I can feel them in my stomach. The days after my second miscarriage bring back one such memory.

It had been a week or two since my second miscarriage. My sister and her family were planning to stay overnight with us on their way through North Carolina. I remember she called and asked if it would be better for them not to stop by in light of our recent miscarriage. "Of course not! We'd love to have you," I responded.

It was true; we do love having them. But she was conscious that the challenge of their visit would not just be the physical work of hosting guests, but the emotional challenge it presented. My sister and I had been pregnant at the same time. Now my baby was dead while hers was still alive.

The evening of their arrival came. I vividly remember standing in the kitchen mixing brownie batter and glancing over at my sister's baby bump. That was all it took. When I realized I was all out of eggs, I briefly mentioned I needed to run to the store then hurried out to the car before anyone could suggest coming with me. Bitter tears flowed down my cheeks as my heart cried out, "Why, God? Why take another baby from me?"

A song began playing in my car as I drove, cried, and prayed. I had never heard this song before and the message was clear and simple: whether your life experiences bring pain or pleasure, come to Jesus with it all. Angry, grieving, and exhausted tears coursed down my cheeks as I sat in the grocery store parking lot and listened. I played the song over and over. I tried to sing along in a quavery, crying voice. I prayed it to the Lord. And during those moments, I realized an incredibly simple, but life altering truth.

Although I didn't know why God allowed this pain and I didn't know how to deal with it, I was convinced that God gave me this pain so I would bring it straight back to him. He gave this exact pain to me so I would use it as a pathway to draw closer to Jesus.

Little did I know how much this lesson would shape me in the next few years. It began as a way to process the pain of a miscarriage. But the Lord continued to impress it on my heart as a way to deal with everything—from small, daily challenges to life-altering heartaches.

I had a habit of seeing hard events as 'trials to endure.' But God has begun to form in my heart the habit of coming to him with hardships instead of stewing over them in my heart. I've discovered over the past few years that through every situation I've brought to Jesus, he has pulled me closer to himself. As a result, the last few years have been the sweetest I've ever experienced in my Christian life.

I look back at that time in the grocery store parking lot as one of the most pivotal moments in my spiritual life. That night God taught me to come to him with everything. He wants me to come. In fact, that's exactly why he puts things in my life—not to see how much I can carry, but to display his glory and strength as he carries me.

What would your life look like if you took every single thing that happened in your life and—instead of stewing over it, shooting an all caps text to your bestie about it, posting about it on social media, or letting your emotions run out of control—you took it prayerfully back to God and said, "Here. Here's what you gave me. I have no clue how to handle it. Can you teach me what to do with it?"

How would your relationship with God be different than it is now? Would you find yourself in closer fellowship with him? I know you would. I know you would because I've seen God do this work in my heart.

When do you come to Jesus?
You come to him all the time and with everything.

What does that look like?

I wrote this book so you can see what it has looked like for me. Everyone's journey will look different, but the end result will be the same: as we come to Jesus, we will become like him.

"Beloved, we are God's children now, and what we will be has not yet appeared; but we know that when he appears we shall be like him, because we shall see him as he is" (1 John 3:2).

What Does It Mean to Come to Jesus?

What does the phrase "come to Jesus" even mean? Is it just a catchy saying with no depth? Or is it something more?

Coming to Jesus means that I look at every single circumstance in my day as an opportunity to run to him with praise and prayer.

It means I don't view the mess my child made, the fight that took place, or the diagnosis I received as an end in themselves, but rather as an opportunity to grow closer to the God who placed these events in my life.

But as I look at my own heart and the habits of those around me, I see a different response and I've become burdened. Here's why:

What do you do when you're frustrated, overwhelmed, or confused? Maybe you send out a frustrated text or call a friend and repeat the terrible events of the past hour. Perhaps you post about it on the internet in a social media group or your timeline. Or maybe you save it all to unload on your best friend or spouse the next time you see them.

No matter which of the above options you choose, the result is the same. We express our angst, perhaps receive sympathetic comments, and we feel validated. But then what happens after we have shared about our hard things? What happens in our hearts—and in the hearts of the people to whom we've complained? Are they encouraged to be faithful in the work God has given them and trust him with the difficulties he's placed in their life?

Or do they move on from the conversation with even more frustration that their husband doesn't get it, their kids don't appreciate anything, and their life is just about as miserable as it gets? Personally, I find the latter response to be my norm.

My friend, I think we're missing out on a big opportunity. Instead of using hard things as a springboard closer to our God we're using them in ways that foster discouragement and bitterness in ourselves and others.

But what if God designed your day today to keep you running back to him? What if he put that exact situation in your life this morning, not so you would have something to tell your friend about, but so you would talk with him about it?

In the following pages, we will look at

- When we should come to Jesus,
- How we come,
- What to do when we don't want to come, &
- Two final ground rules to remember as we come.

I have been praying for you, dear reader.

Although I don't know your name or where you are at this very moment, my Father knows. I am praying that God will use the message of this book to change your heart just as he's been so faithful to change mine.

Christa Threlfall

WHEN DO YOU COME?

Christa Threlfall

Come to Him in Unbelief

There have been many times of unbelief in my life. Times when I didn't believe God was good and in control. Times when I knew he was in control, but I didn't believe he loved me. But there's a specific instance that stands above the rest and it's the story of how my husband, Jonathan began to pursue a Ph.D.

The year was 2010.

Jonathan and I had been married one and a half years, and I had recently given birth to our first child when he broached the topic with a mild suggestion. Something along the lines of, "I think sometime down the road I'd like to take some more classes."

I responded to his suggestion like any sweet, submissive, and trusting wife would: "WHAT?! You've got to be joking! Maybe…as long as it's going to be a long time down the road."

To say I was feeling the stress of new marriage, new ministry, and new mothering responsibilities is a massive understatement.

Fast forward a few months. Jonathan had not yet taken any more classes, in part due to the overwhelming support from his wife. This time he had a different idea: "I think I should pursue a further degree, like a Master of Divinity."

Okay, since I had a freak out session about him taking a class or two, you can guess how I responded to the Master of Divinity idea. "How are you going to find time to do that? How are we going to afford this? I'm never going to see you!" (I feel like it's important to note here that I never exaggerate.)

Between 2011-2012, Jonathan took several local and online classes towards a Master of Divinity degree. With God's help and a boatload of hard work, he excelled in his classes while still managing to be a great daddy and husband. But although he was doing well, it was more of "his thing" than "our thing." God had been working in my heart and convicting me of the sins I displayed in my reaction against Jonathan's idea, so I was truly trying to be a supportive wife by encouraging him in his studies. But if he had given up on the idea of further schooling, I most certainly wouldn't have argued with him. To put it another way: I didn't encourage him to quit, but I certainly would have been the first to throw a party if he had.

So one year later, when he said he was thinking about pursuing a Ph.D., I remember the presence of tears—

feeling like this was going to be the rest of my life: school, school, and more school...*ad infinitum ad nauseam.*

We prayed. We talked.
He researched. I worried.

There were two degrees he was considering: a doctorate of ministry (less time; less money) and a doctorate of philosophy (more time; a whole lot more money). We continued to pray and talk. He continued to research. I continued to worry (with a small dose of prayer).

Then it finally came to this: because of the cost and time difference, he was strongly considering pursuing the doctorate of ministry. It wouldn't be as much pressure on our family and it wouldn't require as much time and intensity from him.

Time out.

Have you ever had the experience when someone tells you about a decision and the reason behind it, but you can tell there's something more there?

Yes. That's the exact experience I had.

Each time Jonathan talked about getting the D.Min. degree instead of the Ph.D., I could tell his heart wasn't in it. When he discussed the rigorous studying required of Ph.D. students, the challenge seemed to motivate him and put a light in his eyes. But when he talked about doing the D.Min., the excitement wasn't there. I knew he had come to this decision because I, as his wife, didn't believe God could get us through the years of schooling, so I was holding him back from what God had called us to do.

I know God allowed us to come to this point for my sake, so that *I* would be the one encouraging him to go for it instead of just dragging myself along until the "torture of school" ceased.

And so I sat in the living room after Jonathan said he was leaning towards the D.Min. for time and financial reasons and shocked both Jonathan and myself when I said, "I really think God wants us to pursue the Ph.D. instead." I remember saying those words and believing them with all my heart. But I also clearly remember thinking, "I cannot believe I'm actually saying this."

It was a collision of fear and faith. Fear because I knew that what I was saying was going to be hard—that the numbers and hours didn't match up. But faith because God allowed us to see that this was exactly the plan he wanted us to pursue.

God brought me to this realization: I could hold my husband back from pursuing God's plan because of my fear and unbelief, or I could come to Jesus, ask him to give me a heart of faith, and seek to be my husband's greatest cheerleader. Fear is easier and much more natural than faith. But faith is so much better than fear, because it's obedience to God's plan and there is always, *always* joy after obedience.

I'm not the best cheerleader that ever existed. But God used this "Ph.D. season" to work in our lives as individuals, as a couple, and as a family. We have seen God provide in energy, health, time, and resources. We have seen God give encouragement through others and we've learned to recognize it as his way of saying, "Yes. This is what I have for you right now. Keep going."

I'm so glad I came to Jesus with my unbelief instead of clinging to my ideas about how much we could handle. I'm so glad he helped me pursue his plan instead of my own. His plan didn't make sense to me, but faith never does. Faith is like leaping across a ravine when you can't see the other side. It's like uprooting your family from their home and moving without a final destination in view. (Read about Abraham's experience in Genesis 12.) It's like building a massive ark when there is no foreseeable need and everyone is making fun of you. (Read Noah's story in Genesis 6.)

Faith doesn't make sense when you're looking with human eyes. And since those happen to be the only eyes I have, faith often doesn't make sense to me. That's why I desperately need Jesus—he's the One who holds my hand when he tells me to jump to the other side I can't see. He's the one who has a destination in mind even when I can't see or understand any part of it. That's why life only makes sense when I bring my unbelief to him, because he's the one who has the end in view.

What about you?

Do you find yourself struggling to trust God in this season of your life? Maybe you struggle to believe that God loves you. Maybe you struggle to believe that he is in control. Bring your unbeliefs to Jesus. His Word is strong enough to stand up to any doubts and his character remains the same whether or not you believe. Come to Jesus with your unbelief.

Come to Him in Loneliness

All of us face times of loneliness, don't we? Whether real or wrongly perceived, the feeling of loneliness can completely discourage you, even though other things in your life may be going well.

I remember a "lonely season" in my life. Living away from family, with a husband in ministry (and enrolled as a seminary student), there were times when I felt incredibly isolated. At one particular time, we had two young children and I remember feeling cloistered away with the demands of babies during the day and my husband busy at night, pressured with work and school.

One Saturday afternoon, while my children napped and my husband studied, I took a walk, called my Mom, and dumped all these troubles on her. (Bless her.) She kindly listened while I talked and cried. I had this sneaking suspicion about what she would say and after I finished talking, she confirmed it with her reply:

"Christa, maybe God wants to use this time in your life to draw you closer to him."

GAH. Tears.
That was not what I wanted to hear.

But I knew in my heart that she was right. I knew this was exactly how God was using this season to change me.

On the inside I was kicking, screaming, and trying to push away from this period of loneliness. But God had a much better and bigger purpose in mind: to use this season to draw me close to himself.

So what did I do?

I prayed. I tried to use the season of loneliness—of wanting someone to talk, laugh, and cry with—as a time to grow deeper in my friendship with God. To take the whole "pray without ceasing" command and let it become a daily reality. To talk, laugh, and cry with the one who made me and put every event in my life.

And what did God do?

Just what he said he would: As I drew closer to him, he became my faithful, never-failing friend. "Draw near to God and he will draw near to you" (James 4:8). In his kindness, he showed me how noisy my soul was and taught me to quiet my heart in his constant, unchanging love. Instead of looking for affirmation and security from other people, I began to find it in him.

But God also did something else when I came to him with my loneliness…something that took a lot longer for me to learn. He expanded my definition of "friendship."

Actually, he blew up my definition and taught me about true love—a love that gives without expecting anything in return. I thought friendship was about finding someone to meet my needs rather than serving others.

The Lord used Philippians 2:3 to confront my selfish way of thinking: "In humility count others more significant than yourselves." God showed me that friendship means denying myself and serving others just as Jesus does for me.

What about you?

I don't know what your relationships look like right now. Maybe you feel like you have a pretty good tribe around you but just have a lonely season every once in awhile. Or maybe you feel like no one even knows you exist. Wherever you find yourself between those two extremes, I know this: God wants you to come to him. When you bring your lonely longings to him, you will find he meets them and changes you in the process. He is the best friend your heart could ever find.

Christa Threlfall

Come to Him
When You Need Advice

People need advice at all ages and stages of life. It's my (probably biased) opinion that one group of people needs advice most desperately—and asks for it most often. Say hello to the new moms. Frazzled by a dizzying array of new decisions (vitamins! doctors! baby gear!), new mamas easily find themselves overwhelmed mentally just when they are most drained physically. What's a girl to do? Here's what I did: I asked my mom friends for advice. Seeking out our friends for advice on prenatal vitamins and where to find the best deal on diapers is incredibly awesome. Go ahead. Poll the audience!

But often we are just as quick to seek advice in major, life-changing issues—breakups, marital struggles, financial stresses, or relational disagreements.

While there certainly is a place for going to godly, experienced people for advice, we cannot substitute any counselor for God.

Keep in mind a couple limitations of getting advice from others:

First, no one else can (or even should) know all the details.

Second, even if a person does know all the details before she offers advice, she is not the one who will live with your decision.

So, what's a person supposed to do? Stop asking advice?

Oh, friend. Do you know that there's someone who knows more about the situation than you do? Do you know that he's aware of all sides of this issue—the timing, sensitivities, difficulties, and hurts? Do you know that he always gives the best "advice?" And that (greatest of all) he lives with you and helps you after you make your decision and take that next step?

Jesus is the only one who fulfills all these roles. "The heart of man plans his ways, but the Lord directs his steps" (Proverbs 16:9). The LORD directs your steps! Not just the ones to get you over the decision hurdle, but the steps afterwards when you deal with the results of your decision. Oh gracious, there is such peace in that, isn't there? We can trust in the Lord!

Whether you need advice for something that affects your next hour or the next twenty years, come to Jesus. Come to him first, before consulting other counselors. Come to him with your questions. Lay it all out before him. Tell him what you want and what you fear. Get in his Word. Listen. Then don't just hear his Word, but go do it. And know that he walks with you and holds your hand through every step.

"For I, the Lord your God, hold your right hand; it is I who say to you, 'Fear not, I am the one who helps you'" (Isaiah 41:13).

Christa Threlfall

Come to Him
When You're Overwhelmed

Merriam-Webster defines "overwhelm" as follows: "Upset, overthrow; to overpower in thought or feeling."

I have often felt incredibly overwhelmed. Sometimes that feeling has come because I've just heard a terribly loud crash from somewhere in my home and a couple of my children are nowhere in sight. Usually, some sort of large mess follows, which tends to involve a hefty degree of cleanup coordination from Mom. That situation falls in the category of "small overwhelmed feelings"—you know, the ones that are pretty quickly resolved, don't take much thought in the process, and often occur multiple times in one day.

But then there's another sort that I put in the category of "large overwhelmed feelings." These deeper feelings might strike when life seems like a series of devastating losses, the whole world seems dismal, or everything appears to be just plain bad. These feelings may come during a genuinely hard period of life, but sometimes they creep up when everything seems fine on the outside, but inside my emotions are in a tumult.

During these times, I cling to the words of Psalm 61:2 (KJV): "From the end of the earth will I cry unto thee, when my heart is overwhelmed: lead me to the rock that is higher than I." Yes! The only relief for an overwhelmed heart is to find rest in God, the solid rock of ages.

"But how do I find rest in God?"

This is the question my heart stammers out. Yes, I'm overwhelmed. And yes, I want to find rest in Christ. But how can I go from a state of overwhelmed feelings (whether large or small) to a state of rest?

The first step to finding rest during overwhelming seasons of life is to stop.

Maybe you're saying, "What? I don't have time to stop! If I could stop, I wouldn't be overwhelmed!" We've all felt that way. Sure, I've never been in your shoes, but I do live in my own, and I understand that cry of protest. But consider this: God hasn't made us to run well without stopping to quiet our souls in him. Perhaps the reason we're so overwhelmed is because we're taking too much on ourselves. Or perhaps we're overwhelmed because we're doing the right things, but trying to do them without God. "Abide in me, and I in you. As the branch cannot bear fruit by itself, unless it abides in the vine, neither can you, unless you abide in me. I am the vine; you are the branches. Whoever abides in me and I in him, he it is that bears much fruit, for apart from me you can do nothing" (John 15:4-5).

We cannot produce anything worthwhile unless we're abiding in Christ—directly connected to him for our life, desires, and joy.

When I feel overwhelmed, the first thing I must do is stop and quiet my soul before God. Sometimes that looks like actually stopping in the middle of a project to pray. Sometimes I feel overwhelmed while homeschooling my children. I will actually stop in the middle of a math problem, hold my child's hand, and say, "We just need to stop and pray that God would help us with this lesson. Mommy is getting upset and we both need God to help us."

But often I stop on the inside, even when I can't stop what I'm doing. It is possible to quiet your heart even though you may not always be able to still your hands.

For example, I might be in the kitchen preparing dinner and thinking about situations that need to be resolved. As I work, I can feel my body growing tense and my mind becoming overwhelmed. My child asks me a question and I snap back an answer, irritated he had the nerve to interrupt my thoughts. My husband comes home and I'm upset he didn't come earlier.

These pressures often assail my heart and home. While it's possible for me to put dinner on hold and go in my room to pray, I usually pray right in the middle of what I'm doing. I may not stop peeling potatoes or unloading the dishwasher, but I tell my thoughts to stop and take a chill pill while I hash things out with God. I list out all the things making me feel anxious. I tell God why I'm worried and ask him to help me think correctly and rest in him. I pray God's Words back to him: "When my heart is overwhelmed: lead me to the rock that is higher than I." (Psalm 61:2) Sometimes that journey to the Rock looks like me talking to myself the whole way. "No, Christa, stop worrying about that situation. God has promised to take care of you and he will work it out in his perfect time."

I have discovered, though, that there is rest to be found at the Rock that is higher than I. I've never found it where I like to dwell—devising strategies to fix problems and thinking about a myriad of issues. The rest is found only when I come to Jesus. Until I come to him, I'm too overwhelmed trying to plan out how I can do everything.

"Rest is found only when I come to Jesus."

Here's the truth: I can't do everything, nor should I try to. But Jesus can! He can do every thing that needs to be done —down to the last detail! And he can work through me as I follow what he's called me to do.

When I'm working while abiding in Christ, I'm not frenzied or overwhelmed. Instead, I'm working from this solid, stabilizing truth: "Come to me, all who labor and are heavy laden, and I will give you rest. Take my yoke upon you, and learn from me, for I am gentle and lowly in heart, and you will find rest for your souls. For my yoke is easy, and my burden is light" (Matthew 11:28-29).

There is rest found in Jesus. Come to him when you're overwhelmed.

Christa Threlfall

Come to Him When You're Struggling With a Life Change

Have you ever been through a difficult life change?

Maybe your change was something unexpected—a job loss, a crushing diagnosis, or the sudden loss of someone you love. Or maybe your change was one you actually chose—a new job, the birth or adoption of a child, or moving to a new place.

Change in life is inevitable. And it seems that, for us as humans, change and struggle often go hand in hand.

There have been times I thought I was doing well with a life change (such as those first months of marriage), but as years go by, I realize just how much I struggled through it all. Looking back, I know it was only the Lord's grace that kept my husband and I serving and loving each other through the first months of marriage and ministry! Change is hard.

What do you do when you're struggling with a life change? Here's what I tend to do: play the blame game.

Who's at fault for this change?
My husband? *"Okay, babe, I'm officially annoyed with you."*
Me? *"Why do I have to be so stupid?"*
Someone else? *"Argh. People are so frustrating sometimes!"*

Yet while I blame myself and others, I ignore God, the real change-maker. And until I come to him—the one who is ultimately in charge of every change—I never experience peace. I will never come to terms with either the change or the earthly force behind that change until I bring my struggles to God, lay them at his feet, surrender my foolish thoughts of "I'm okay. I can handle this." and instead realize that I'm never "okay" when I try to handle life without God.

I will never forget the way God so gently taught me this lesson soon after a move when I was about chest-deep in struggles. My response to these struggles was affecting the way I viewed my husband, children, God, and others. I kept thinking, "If we had never moved, I wouldn't be struggling like this!"

It was mid-March and I was on a chilly walk outdoors. As I walked, I came up to a large pile of dirt dug up from a nearby field. There, on the very top of that mound, a single daffodil was blooming. Have you ever heard the phrase "Bloom where you're planted?" That phrase instantly came to my mind and God gently convicted my heart.

That afternoon, God gave me a powerful visual lesson. By showing me that flower blooming on uprooted soil, he reminded me that he doesn't call me to grow only when my "life-soil" is exactly the way I want it. He calls me to grow right where he plants me—no matter who is or isn't around and no matter how different this location is from where I used to live.

Furthermore, my struggles don't spring from where I am, but from who I am. I wasn't picking fights with my husband because we were in a different geographical location. Instead, that life change of moving revealed the many struggles that were already lodged deep inside my heart.

We must come to Jesus during life changes. We are incapable of handling them on our own. The sooner we come to terms with this and remember our desperate need for God, the sooner we receive his strength and grace to grow through difficult changes.

What about you?

What change is God leading you through right now? Rest in him. Just as a sleeping baby completely trusts his mother to safely carry him to the crib, trust your heavenly Father to carry you through this season of life. He made you and created you to go through—and grow through—this change. He won't drop you. Trust in him.

Christa Threlfall

Come to Him
When You're Not Thankful

How do you come to Jesus when there are things in your life that you hate? What do you do with those verses that tell you to give thanks in all things? "Giving thanks always and for everything to God the Father in the name of our Lord Jesus Christ" (1 Thessalonians 5:20).

I have vivid memories of the first time God arrested my heart with this verse. I was lying on the couch, resting from a recent miscarriage and praying for God's help when the above verse came to mind.

Give thanks always?
For everything?

At the moment, that command seemed so far out of my reach, it would have been laughable if the idea wasn't so painful.

As I lay there thinking through this verse, I cried to God, "How can you tell me to give thanks for the loss of my child? This is not a good thing! How can you expect me to thank you for something so heartbreaking?"

I didn't know. And to be honest, I didn't really want to find out. But I decided I could be honest with God.

"God, I'm not thankful that I lost my baby. You tell me to give thanks and I really want to obey you. So I'm going to say thanks, but you know my heart isn't in it. Help me to learn how to be thankful through this."

Even now—five years later—it hurts to put this into words. And even now, I can't look at that situation and say, "I am so thankful that happened!"

It was hard. And it's still painful.

But here's what I've learned through God's kind and patient teaching: *I can give thanks for everything.*

Not because everything is good. But because there is a good God behind it, in it, and through it.

Giving thanks for difficult, heartbreaking things requires that I look beyond what I think is good and trust that God knows what's best. I have to get past my desires and agenda and look with faith on God's plan.

Sometimes I have looked back and seen how God gave me a thankful heart when I didn't even think gratitude was possible. Even now there are still areas I take to him and say, "God, thank you for this struggle, even though I don't like it or understand it. Help me to be truly thankful for it because it comes from your good and wise hand."

You know what's so great about giving thanks to God for everything? It keeps me running back to him.

So whether it's something I recognize immediately as a blessing, or something I instinctively view as a trial, I can take it back to the God who gave it to me. And I can be thankful.

What about you?

I don't know what is going on in your heart today. I'm sure there are hard things in your life that you secretly (or maybe not so secretly) wish would vanish. In fact, if you were God, these are things you never would have allowed in your life in the first place. Is God good and worthy of your thanks even through this?

Giving thanks for all things does not look like a fake smile and praise hands in all situations. Instead, giving thanks requires you to ask hard questions of yourself and God that can't be answered without careful thought and quiet prayer.

Will you take your struggle to God and ask him to help you be grateful for his sovereign will? Will you ask him for eyes of faith to see beyond the heartbreak?

He can help you. Come to Jesus when you're not thankful.

Christa Threlfall

Come to Him
When You've Failed

This morning held a fresh example of failure.

I was sitting in my child's room—attempting to help him realize that the offense he had just committed was indeed a display of sinful anger, and deserved repentance. However, my child was not willing to verbalize his offense. He obviously needed my help crafting his confession of the crime, so I began to pummel him with a series of rapid-fire questions.

"How did you respond when your blanket fell on the floor?"
Silence.
"You were …"
Still silence.
"Were you happy?"
"No."
"No, you weren't happy. You were _____?"

More silence.
"You weren't happy, you were what?"
Silence again.
My voice rose in pitch and volume: "You were...? Angry! You were angry, weren't you?!"

Immediately (yes, I do mean immediately), the Holy Spirit convicted me of the hypocritical—not to mention foolish—behavior I had just displayed. How can I teach my child to overcome anger when I can't even conquer it myself?

"Honey, I'm so sorry. Mommy was angry at you just then. Will you forgive me?"

My child forgave me, and we finished our conversation by praying together and asking God to help us overcome the anger in our hearts.

Failure. It's something I face constantly. Some failures I stumble into daily, like the one I mentioned above. Other failures are easily (even if painfully) fixed. Still some failures are life-changing. What does it look like to come to Jesus when I fail? It looks like humility and brokenness.

Humility because I've done wrong. I've messed up. I've sinned. I know it was wrong. Others know it was wrong. And I'm coming to you, God, because I need your forgiveness.

Brokenness because I can't make this right. I'm the one who brought harm and hurt to this situation. I am incapable of resolving it without help. On my own, I will continue to bring more pain. It is only through Jesus that I can have wisdom to know what to do and strength to carry it out.

What's the alternative?

What's the alternative to coming to Jesus when I fail? The alternative is continuing to pound away at life on my own. The reason I failed in the first place is because I moved away from God and tried to do life on my own. If I continue to live life without the humility and brokenness that make me cling to Jesus, I am guaranteed to live a life without forgiveness and true wisdom.

On the other hand, coming to Jesus with my failures guarantees that I will find forgiveness because of his work on the cross. It means that his wisdom is at my disposal! It means that his strength is always present, out-matching my every weakness.

I can continue on my own path of brokenness and failure, or I can come to Jesus in brokenness with my failures. The choice is mine.

The choice is also yours. Will you come to Jesus with your failures today?

Come to Him When the Future Looks Uncertain

First, let's be honest: When can we ever have certainty about the future on this earth? Obviously, never.

But while the future is always technically uncertain, there are some times in life when it actually looks more uncertain than at other times. One such time stands out in my mind.

It all started on Sunday morning, May 1, 2016. I was just shy of twenty weeks pregnant with our fourth baby. I woke up and went for a slow 2 mile run. (Nothing unusual there as I have continued running throughout all my pregnancies, sometimes the night before giving birth.) As I came home and started getting ready for church, I noticed a growing pain in my lower back. With my last pregnancy, I began having round ligament pain, so I assumed that was the issue and continued my morning routine. As the pain increased, I thought about taking medicine, but instead decided to try to massage it out. At this point, I didn't think anything was wrong, but I did tell my kids that my back was hurting and even texted Jonathan (who was already at church) to tell him I was in pain.

There were a couple big "wait-a-minute" moments that made me think this was something more than back pain. The first such moment happened when I was moving so much through my back pain and thought, "Wow, this reminds me of labor!" Of course, I quickly discounted that thought since I was only 20 weeks pregnant.

The second was when I felt a small gush of fluid. "Wait. Did my water just break?" My back pain was still very present. It was time to leave for church, but scary questions were running through my mind: "Is this just normal back pain? Was that really my water breaking? Do I need to go to the hospital?"

I called Jonathan, but there was no answer. He was in the same music practice I was supposed to be in. I decided to call the nurse and tell her what was going on.

"This is my fourth baby and I think my water just broke." (I figured she'd be more likely to believe me once she knew this wasn't my first rodeo.) Towards the end of the conversation, my pain was increasing. The nurse put me on hold while she talked with Labor & Delivery, then came back on the line to tell me to drive to the hospital where they were expecting me. When she started giving me the address of where to go, I was in so much pain and said in a very irritated voice that I could just figure it out. That was my third "wait-a-minute" moment.

By now it was around 10:15 AM. Jonathan was in the middle of teaching Sunday School, Anna Grace was organizing a card-making-party with Nate since Mommy was in so much pain, and Miles was throwing a couple temper tantrums in rapid succession. I was debating whether this pain was worth pulling Jonathan from the middle of his class when I got the urge to push. And then it came again.

I texted Jonathan: "I think my water might have broken. I just got off the phone with the nurse and think I should go to the hospital to get checked out just in case. I need you to come home."

He texted back: "On my way."

(He told me later that he filled out the rest of the blanks in his handout, gave it to one of the guys in class, and said "Christa needs my help. Will you finish this lesson for me?" I always knew I married a good man, but this event just confirmed it times 100.)

I explained to my kids that I needed to go to the doctor because I thought their baby sister might be trying to come. As soon as I said this, my kids responded to the information in their typical manner:
Miles (2 years old) didn't understand and was completely unfazed. Nate (4) asked if I wanted a band-aid for my pain and said, "Mommy, I've had that back pain before." Anna

Grace (6) shrieked, "THE BABY'S COMING?!?!" and immediately ran to another room and fell prostrate on the carpet.

Right before I left, Anna Grace gave me a hug goodbye. She wouldn't look me in the eye, but I could tell her eyes were red from crying. I lifted her chin in my hands and said, "Honey, whatever happens I want you to remember this: God is good. And we can trust him. Okay? You have to remember that." We both cried, then I left them with some dear friends from our church while Jonathan & I headed to the hospital.

As soon as we got settled in the hospital room, a nurse listened to our baby girl's heartbeat. To our surprise and delight, it was strong. The nurse strapped a device on me to monitor my now-weakening contractions. The doctor on call was notified, and I was relieved to hear that it was the OB doctor I had been going to for over five years. Before she arrived, I had several large gushes of fluid—so much, in fact, that the nurse doubted that a test was necessary to determine whether it was amniotic fluid.

When the doctor arrived, she used an ultrasound to see the baby and my fluid level. My baby girl looked great, she said, and—to our surprise—that my fluid level was not excessively low. Because there was still a good amount of fluid surrounding baby, she wanted to do a test to see if it truly was amniotic fluid leaking.

While Jonathan and I waited for the results of the test, I had a couple more large gushes of fluid. I told him I would love to think my water hadn't broken and our baby was safe, but I couldn't imagine what else this fluid could be.

My doctor came back and confirmed the results of the test: It was amniotic fluid. My water had broken. And I was only 20 weeks pregnant.

"You have three options," she explained. "You can expedite delivery, you can go home now, or you can spend the night and leave in the morning."

Wait, what? Jonathan and I glanced at each other in shock. These didn't sound like reasonable options at all.

I asked my doctor if anything would be done to save the baby if we expedited delivery. She said nothing would be done. "So I can either expedite delivery and be certain my baby will die or I can wait to see if she stays in the womb a little longer to increase her chance of living?"

My doctor confirmed that those were my options. But she stressed that if I didn't expedite delivery, I ran the risk of infection which could lead to a hysterectomy for me or cerebral palsy for my baby.

Here is where I must stop to praise God for the wisdom he gives. Based on the previous ultrasound, we knew (and our doctor knew) that the baby girl inside me was strong and healthy. She showed no signs of distress. Despite the possibility of infection and other dire outcomes, we made a decision—not based on what we feared could happen, but on what we knew was true.

What did we know to be true? We knew that God had given us this baby. We knew that whether we had her for twenty more minutes or twenty more years, we had the responsibility to protect her. Since there were no signs of distress, we could not in good conscience expedite a delivery that would lead to her death, despite my doctor's advice to do so.

I was still leaking fluid, so we decided it was best to spend the night closely monitored in the hospital. My doctor told me that I could stay at home until I was twenty-three weeks pregnant, at which point I would be hospitalized and put on bedrest until the baby was born. I was immediately given antibiotics to stave off infection.

When Jonathan and I were alone in the room, we cried and prayed together. We were so scared. Scared for our baby. Scared because it looked like we would lose her that day. I was so glad to have him pray with me as the only prayer I could sob was, "Jesus, help."

I spent the night alone in the hospital while Jonathan went home to be with our three older kids. At first, spending time alone seemed like a terrible prospect, but it proved to be a special time to pray and cry out to God. As I lay in bed, God reminded me of the words I had told my daughter that morning: *"God is good. And we can trust him."*

That night, God reminded me that **his goodness remains**

unchanged despite my changing circumstances. And I cried out and begged him for a faith that desperately clings to truths about him even when my heart and circumstances scream lies that he doesn't love me and has lost control. My hardships do not diminish his goodness. He isn't good only when I experience good. He isn't in control only when I feel that my circumstances are under control. He is good all the time.

By late Sunday evening, both my contractions and amniotic fluid leaking had stopped (without intervention or medication). I started guzzling water like crazy in case it might help replace some of the fluid I had just lost.

I was discharged late Monday morning with a prescription for antibiotics, but no restrictions on my activity. When I questioned why I would be hospitalized and put on bedrest at twenty-three weeks but not at twenty weeks, she responded that "everyone is betting against this baby" since my labor has already commenced and the baby isn't viable. After consulting two other doctors who advised me not to resume my normal activities, we decided I should be on bedrest for two weeks until my next appointment when I would find out further information on my baby and the fluid level. We learned there was a very small chance that my amniotic sac could reseal, so we began earnestly praying for God to work a miracle over the next weeks.

Two Weeks of Waiting

During this two week period, I did a lot of sitting and lying down. Sweet friends from our church and community started bringing meals and coming over daily to watch my kids, clean toilets, do laundry, serve meals, and break up the inevitable fights between three small children.

I tried to parent from the couch. *Very difficult.*

I continued drinking obscene amounts of water. *Difficult to accomplish and stay on the couch for long.*

I developed an itchy rash from sitting and lying down so much. *Ugh & Yuck.*

Jonathan attempted to work, study for his Ph. D. classes, clean the house, and take care of the kids without much of any help from me. *HARD, hard.*

We wrestled through questions we didn't know how to answer: Am I going to begin leaking amniotic fluid again? Is this baby going to survive until twenty-three weeks? How will our family make it if I'm hospitalized and on bedrest from twenty-three weeks until this baby is born?

Through the whole period of waiting—bedrest for me; extra work for Jonathan and so many of our friends—this was the lesson God kept lovingly pressing into my soul: *"I am good. You can trust me."*

Was it an accident that my scheduled Bible reading was in Psalms during my first week of bedrest? Clearly not. God directed my heart to Psalm 62:5-8 during those first few days:

"For God alone, O my soul, wait in silence, for my hope is from him. He only is my rock and my salvation, my fortress; I shall not be shaken. On God rests my salvation and my glory; my mighty rock, my refuge is God. Trust in him at all times, O people; pour out your heart before him; God is a refuge for us."

I knew that regardless of the outcome of these two weeks, I wanted my heart to be resting in God and trusting in his will, whatever that turned out to be.

Isaiah 26:3-4 was also a rich blessing to me:

"You keep him in perfect peace whose mind is stayed on you, because he trusts in you. Trust in the LORD forever, for the LORD GOD is an everlasting rock."

I love these verses because they remind me that peace comes when my mind is dwelling on God. And my mind can only dwell on God (instead of problems and the unknown) when I'm trusting in him. Truth! It is so important to speak truth from God's Word to your soul when your mind and emotions are shouting otherwise!

God also impressed his tender love on our family during these weeks. He loved us through our time in his Word and he loved us through his body, the church. We were often brought to tears when our sweet friends and church family sent text messages, brought meals, gave personal gifts, and made grocery store runs. I only wore mascara two days through that whole time because my tears kept scrawling black streaks down my face. I wasn't even safe writing thank you notes, as I would think about the way people had shown such kind care for us and cry with gratefulness at the way God was tenderly loving us through our time of need.

Our two weeks of waiting finally came to an end, so Jonathan and I headed to a follow-up appointment with a new doctor for high-risk pregnancies. I went in with mixed emotions: I was happy I hadn't experienced any more leaking, nervous at what they might discover, and at peace knowing that God was going to help us through the future just as he had faithfully guided through the last weeks.

Verdict? Our baby girl was strong and healthy, my fluid level was abundant, and it seemed that my amniotic sac had resealed, so there were no restrictions on my activity and no need to plan for early hospitalization.

Excuse me, what?

Jonathan and I left the appointment overwhelmed with gratitude, but somewhat befuddled—like we had just been on a terribly wild roller coaster that came to a jerky stop. We prayed and thanked God for answering many prayers and I walked out of the hospital as if I hadn't been on bedrest over the past two weeks. Four months later, Karis Faith (our little miracle baby) was born—one day past her due date, just to re-emphasize the fact that God is in control and worthy of my trust.

God is worth trusting—not because Karis was born safely —but because his character is trustworthy. He is trustworthy, no matter what your future holds or how uncertain it appears. If I had not come to him in surrender during that night in the hospital, the end result would not have been so precious.

As it is, God gave me the grace to release my tight hold on my baby, and entrust her into the hands of my kind Father. So when he allowed her to be born safely, it was all just as it was from the beginning of my pregnancy—a gracious gift.

I'm more aware than ever that there are no guarantees—in my life or anyone else's. The only guarantees you and I have are the promises given in God's Word. He is a good Father who loves you so much that he gave Jesus to die for you and take the punishment for your sins. He is a God who is worthy of your trust.

I don't know what you're going through today. I don't know whether your future seems like it's in control or whether you feel like it's spiraling into chaos. Either way, remember this: Our future is in control, but it's not in our control. It's in the hands of someone so much better, wiser, and stronger than we are.

So come to him. He is a faithful, trustworthy Father. Bring him your uncertain future.

Christa Threlfall

Come to Him With Praise

Everybody loves this one, right? It seems easy to come to Jesus with praise because it means good things are happening. We all love good things!

But we don't always attribute those good things to Jesus. Many times I find myself forgetting I've ever experienced good things until life begins to get difficult. And then I think, "I wish life was back to the way it was last year!" (Except I forget that last year I didn't think things were so great either.) The grass always does seem greener on the other side, doesn't it?

What does it look like to come to Jesus with praise? It looks like this: "Jesus, thank you for this."

That's it. No strings attached. No extra clauses like, "but I sure wish you would have done this too!" or "maybe next time you could remember that prayer request for the pay raise!"

Coming to Jesus with praise looks like me taking time to remember that all I deserve is eternal punishment. It means that I stop looking at myself, people around me, and things in general. Instead, I lift my stubborn gaze to look on Christ alone, the one who took my punishment for me. And as I gaze on him, I worship. I tell him how good he is to love me, an unworthy sinner. I praise him for his generosity that he graciously bestows on his own creation. I thank him for now—yes, right now!—instead of thinking pessimistic thoughts about tomorrow.

Coming to Jesus with praise means that I'm more focused on him than on myself.

When I focus on myself, I can fool myself into thinking that I'm praising God when really I'm just expressing my self-centeredness. My thoughts can become obsessed with my desires and needs, my family and relationships, my goals, and my problems. That false "praise" makes everything all about me instead of all about God. Instead, I need to redirect my gaze to him. What is he doing? Not just in my heart today, but in the world? What has he been working on since time began? How is he advancing his cause? How can I praise him for what he's doing large scale, not just in my life?

Of course, coming to Jesus with praise means praising him for the ways He's daily working in my life. I want to praise God for what he's doing in my heart right now—for the way he gave patience when I wanted to get angry with my children and the humility he gave to apologize to my husband.

But coming to Jesus with praise means worshipping him for the work he's doing all around the world—not just in my life today, but ever since time began. Often I'm so focused on the minute details of my life that I don't even consider the ways God is at work outside of my realm of experience.

Here are some areas to praise God for that will help lift your eyes off yourself and strengthen your faith in God's control:

- the fact that his holy Word remains, despite the many attempts to destroy it over the years
- the faithfulness he gave to saints in the Bible (and so many believers since then) and the encouragement their testimony is to the church today
- the way he's advancing his church all around the world
- the promises he's fulfilling for believers in heaven.

Here's what I'm learning: **coming to Jesus with praise means it's all about him and what he's doing, not all about me and what I'm receiving.** Praise is not limited to how I feel or experience, because it's focused on who he is. And because Jesus never changes, this means I can come to him with praise all the time.

"I will bless the LORD at all times;
his praise shall continually be in my mouth.
My soul makes its boast in the LORD;
let the humble hear and be glad.
Oh, magnify the LORD with me,
and let us exalt his name together!"
Psalm 34:1-3

Christa Threlfall

HOW DO YOU COME?

The Requirement for Coming

"Come to me, all who labor and are heavy laden, and I will give you rest. Take my yoke upon you, and learn from me, for I am gentle and lowly in heart, and you will find rest for your souls" (Matthew 11:28-29).

Whom does Jesus invite to come to him?

Those who labor and are heavy laden.
Those who are worn out and weary with life.
Those who are stressed out and can't take any more.

The only requirement for a truly rested soul is to come to Jesus. When my heart feels burdened down and weary, my first response is to look for a way out. But soul rest is not found in a change of pace; it is only found in Jesus Christ.

Why? Because Jesus died for your sin. "Christ Jesus is the one who died—more than that, who was raised—who is at the right hand of God, who indeed is interceding for us" (Romans 8:34).

So what is required to come to him?
Simply abandoning our sinful ways and turning in faith to him.

I say "simply" because it's the only thing, not because it's the easiest.

Before I can come to Jesus, I must do something extremely difficult—something that's impossible without God's help and that goes against my very nature. While Jesus invites all who are weary and heavy laden to come to him, the requirement for coming to him is nothing short of putting yourself to death. "I have been crucified with Christ. It is no longer I who live, but Christ who lives in me. And the life I now live in the flesh I live by faith in the Son of God, who loved me and gave himself for me" (Galatians 2:20).

Of course, it's not an actual physical death we're talking about, but I think it's even harder than that. This death Jesus is talking about is something that results in me denying myself (my ambitions and achievements) in favor of following him, seeking to fulfill his mission instead of my own.

Denying myself means that I look at all my pursuits, accomplishments, and knowledge as not just second in command, but actually worthless. This is what Paul talks about when he makes a list of his family background, schooling, and achievements, and sums them all up with this statement: "Whatever gain I had, I counted as loss for the sake of Christ. Indeed, I count everything as loss because of the surpassing worth of knowing Christ Jesus my Lord. For his sake I have suffered the loss of all things and count them as rubbish, in order that I may gain Christ and be found in him, not having a righteousness of my own that comes from the law, but that which comes through faith in Christ, the righteousness from God that depends on faith—that I may know him and the power of his resurrection, and may share his sufferings, becoming like him in his death, that by any means possible I may attain the resurrection from the dead" (Philippians 3:7-11).

Paul's focus in these verses is not on himself at all. He has counted the cost of denying himself and has discovered that it's worth giving up absolutely everything he has in order to know Jesus Christ.

But here's the part you might never hear: there is joy when you deny yourself and come to Jesus. It doesn't look like a fake smile in the midst of a life full of drudgery: "*I might look completely miserable, but I'm secretly joyful!*"

No, dear friend. God's joy is one that starts in the core of your soul as you deny yourself and come to him, recognizing that only Jesus is the way, the truth, and the life. (John 14:6) There is no other religion, pursuit, relationship, or achievement that could ever fulfill your heart as he does. And his joy doesn't stay inside your soul. Instead it comes spilling out and is clearly evident to everyone around you—your spouse, children, co-workers, neighbors, and friends. "May the God of hope fill you with all joy and peace in believing, so that by the power of the Holy Spirit you may abound in hope" (Romans 15:13).

It is worth denying yourself in order to come to Jesus and receive the perfect rest and joy only he can give. He is the only one who can grant you forgiveness from sin and a lasting peace that is only available when you believe in his perfect son, Jesus Christ. "Peace I leave with you; my peace I give to you. Not as the world gives do I give to you. Let not your hearts be troubled, neither let them be afraid" (John 14:27).

Give Jesus the hard things you're trying to carry. Learn from his gentle heart. And experience the soul-rest only he can give.

Daily Coming

My daily routine of coming to Jesus is just what most routines are: fairly consistent & mostly mundane. It begins with a groggy, "Good morning, God. Thanks for waking me up today." Then I get out of bed and get my Bible for a time of reading and more prayer. But that's only the beginning (and the most controlled) part of my day. This part of my routine typically happens before the four children who live in my home are awake. It's a necessary part of my daily coming to the Lord, but it's habitual and certainly not spontaneous.

The times I find most difficult to come to the Lord are when I—well, to be totally honest—completely forget. When my two boys begin fighting over a plastic whistle, my baby cries even when being held twenty-four/seven, my daughter needs help with her piano practice, I get a difficult text message, and the oatmeal overflows in the microwave. During these times, my overwhelm status maxes out and I completely forget about prayer.

And then there are times when I remember that I should pray, but dismiss prayer as irrelevant to my situation. As in, I can't stop to pray right now; I need to act!

But I've discovered—through times of foolishly trying it out—that the longer I act without taking things to Jesus the higher my stress level rises. On the other hand, when I come to the Lord before any stress begins, then come to him the moment difficulties start and ask him for help as I respond—well, I come to the end of that incident and discover I'm right where I want to be: close to Jesus. And if I do that all day long, then I'll find that all those potentially stressful incidents have simply been tools to remind me of my need for Christ.

Before I go to sleep, I love to end my days talking with Jesus—talking about the ways he helped me through the day's events (in order to praise him and remind myself), asking him to forgive me for the ways I failed him and others, and praying for people he brings to mind.

This is what it looks like to come to Jesus in the daily struggles. It's an intentional routine, a practiced habit. It means you train your mind to go to him first thing in the morning, remind your heart to run to him during each event that takes place—whether a struggle or joy. And you make him your last thought before you go to sleep.

Life-Altering Coming

Sometimes God puts events in my life that are not of the "daily struggle" variety, but are life-altering. Many times, these life-altering struggles come in the form of loss—perhaps of a relationship, job, health, or the life of someone I love. The Lord shepherds all his children through these life-altering events, but sometimes we run from his shepherding.

These three habits have helped me come to Jesus during such life-altering events:

1. Hold on to verses about God's character

God's character is the only part of your world that never changes. Therefore, it is the most stabilizing thing you can think about, especially during times of upheaval in your heart and mind. Each time my heart is hit with a trial, my mind reels with the changing nature of life. *Nothing is steady! I can't trust anything or anyone! Everything is falling apart!*

Yet while everything I know may be falling apart, God remains the same. "God is our refuge and strength, a very present help in trouble. Therefore we will not fear though the earth gives way, though the mountains be moved into the heart of the sea" (Psalm 46:1-2).

One practical way to come to Jesus during life-altering trials is to memorize and recite verses that describe God's character and actions—who he is and what he does. Verses like Psalm 119:68, "You are good and do good; teach me your statutes." and Psalm 40:11, "As for you, O Lord, you will not restrain your mercy from me; your steadfast love and your faithfulness will ever preserve me!"

Hold on to truths about God's character and you'll find your faith restored and your heart renewed.

2. Preach truth to your heart.

Consider what happens when you go through a life-altering trial. You start thinking about it, and your thoughts may be unhelpful or untrue. *"Why did this happen? God doesn't love me. I've been so faithful! Why would God allow this? What did I do to deserve this?"*

If it's a public sort of trial (as opposed to a private matter), other people begin talking with you about it. Like your own thoughts, much of what they say may be unhelpful or untrue as well. *"I can't believe this happened. This must be because of your sin. I don't understand why God allowed this into your life."*

Proverbs 10:19 comes to mind: "When words are many, transgression is not lacking."

What do you do when you and others begin pumping thoughts through your head, or when you hear or think something that casts doubt on the goodness of God?

We must bear in mind that what we allow our minds to dwell on determines our beliefs and actions. We become what we think. On one hand, if we constantly worry about the problems around us, our lives will reflect that inner turmoil. However, when we discipline our minds to focus on the unchanging character of Christ, our actions reflect his life.

It's like this promise in Isaiah: "You keep him in perfect peace whose mind is stayed on you, because he trusts in you. Trust in the LORD forever, for the LORD GOD is an everlasting rock" (Isaiah 26:3-4). God promises perfect peace when we fix our thoughts on him. How does that work? When we rehearse truths about God, we demonstrate our trust in Him. So every time that nagging worry comes to your mind, use it as a reminder to bring your concern to the Lord in prayer. Why worry about something when your all powerful, infinitely loving Father will take care of it?

When we rest in truth about God, we gain peace instead of anxiety. But this peace only comes as we discipline our minds to combat lies with the truth. How crucial it is to take this opportunity to preach truth to our hearts! Use the verses you're clinging to about God's character to pump life into your mind and preach truth to your heart.

3. Listen to music that nourishes your soul

At several points in my life, God's Word through music has been the means of reviving my sorrow-numbed heart. In fact, there are some songs which immediately remind me of a particular trial, and the comfort God gave me through that song.

When you're in the trenches of a life-altering trial, it is essential to fill your mind with truths from God's Word. While you might not be able to read and listen to the Bible all the time, there is a way you can regularly fill your mind with God's truth: listen to music that feeds your soul! Even when your hands are busy doing something else, you can preach truth to your heart through the ministry of music.

Listen to songs that exalt the name, character, and acts of Jesus Christ. Listen to songs with Scriptural lyrics—or, even better, lyrics that are Scripture. Listen to songs that tell of God's blessings through trials, his constant presence throughout all of life, and the responsibility of every believer to remain faithful to him through the good and hard times of life.

Worship, sing, and pray to the one who has brought this trial into your life.

When You Don't Want To Come

Sometimes I find myself struggling with something I know I should take to Jesus, but at the same time, I continue to resist taking it to him. Through times of prayer, God has shown me that I usually resist bringing my struggles to him because there's a lie I'm believing about God's character or my abilities.

Here are four lies I frequently believe that cause me to stop coming to Jesus with my struggles:

Lie #1: "I've Got This."

This is the first and most prevalent lie regarding problems. It's incredibly deceptive because we usually don't even say it, either out loud or in our hearts. But there are a few key ways you can know if you're believing this lie.

• You don't pray about it. Believing the "I've got this" lie means I think that I don't need help. And if I don't need help, I won't talk to God about it.

- You become stressed out trying to figure out the answer. (See above about the lack of prayer.)
- You become consumed with the problem. It negatively affects your thoughts, emotions, and relationships.

The biggest problem with believing the "I've got this" lie is that it diverts my attention from God. It's not that I intentionally think I don't need him; instead, I do everything as if I'm the most capable person in the universe (because apparently sometimes I think I am). And then I experience all the effects mentioned above and realize maybe I'm not the greatest at discovering solutions to problems after all. Go figure.

Lie #2: "I Shouldn't Be Struggling With This."

I told myself this lie when we moved from our first ministry in North Carolina. In the Lord's providence, he moved us to Richmond, Virginia—the same church where my dad was a pastor and my sister and her family attended. While I was so excited to live near family, I was heartbroken to leave our dear church family and the city where my husband and I had brought home our four babies. Instead of frankly acknowledging my grief and taking it to the Lord for help, I tried to suppress it by reasoning, "I shouldn't be struggling with this! I'm near family now!" My capstone argument was, "My husband isn't struggling with this, so I should be fine too!"

If you want to make your problem ten times more difficult to handle, just start believing this lie: I shouldn't be struggling! I hate this lie because I've personally experienced its terrible effects many times. Here's how it goes:

- A problem begins.
- I begin processing it, find it hard not to feel hurt, and instinctively respond with, "Why is this a big deal? I shouldn't be struggling!"
- I stop trying to work through it because "it's not a big deal and I obviously shouldn't be struggling with it," so just stop it already.

The biggest problem with believing the "I shouldn't be struggling with this" lie is that I forget who I am. I forget I'm a sinner who has weaknesses, hurts, phobias, and a host of other issues. Instead, I respond in pride, reasoning I'm beyond such simple struggles as the one I'm experiencing. Instead of taking the problem back to the Lord who allowed it into my life, I pretend it's not an issue anymore. By then, it's usually grown five times the size it was when I tried to sweep it under the rug.

In the case of my struggle with our move, it was around this time (when I had all but turned into a crazy person) that I finally asked my husband for help. It didn't sound quite like a gentle plea for his benevolent assistance. More like an ugly cry paired with my blurting out, "I just don't even understand why I'm struggling with this! You're not struggling! Why aren't you having a hard time? Why is this so difficult for me?!"

At that point, my husband and God were the voices of reason in my life, reminding me to acknowledge the problem, draw close to Jesus, and bring my lack of problem solving skills to his very capable and caring heart. And God is so kind. He brought such sweet relief when I brought my hurting, struggling heart to Jesus, the one who knows it best.

It is only when I acknowledge my struggles as what they are (genuine, bona fide problems for which I need God's help) that I can receive God's kind, loving care.

Lie #3: Big vs. Little (also known as: my trial isn't as hard as someone else's trial)

Ah, yes. The comparison struggle. I know it all too well. It starts like this:

A friend of mine receives a cancer diagnosis. Their world seems in a standstill, while also moving at breakneck speed.

Meanwhile, an acquaintance of mine says something unkind to me. While I initially feel hurt, I attempt to brush it off with the reasoning of, "This isn't as hard as cancer, for crying out loud. I need to just get over it."

Or maybe your struggle is cancer and you find yourself looking at someone else's trial, thinking, "Well, my cancer isn't as hard as their _____."

Do you know the core problem of this lie? I'm not looking to Jesus for relief. Instead, I'm trying to find relief in the fact that, "it could be worse." Yes, that's true! It could always be worse! But true relief is never found in comparing my trial to someone else's: True relief doesn't come when you say, "My problems aren't as bad as theirs, thank goodness!" Instead, true relief is found when I bring my struggle to Jesus.

Here's something that helps me when I start believing this lie: "Casting all your anxieties on him, because he cares for you" (1 Peter 5:7). Specifically, it's that little word "all."

Think about it: God doesn't ask for only big cares. He doesn't tell me to give him the life-altering stuff and work through the petty, daily struggles on my own. He says to cast all my cares on him. Now that's a command I can get behind! Hallelujah, right?

Sometimes when I take my struggle to him, I find myself praying, "God, this is a little thing and I'm embarrassed to be struggling with it. But I am struggling! And I really need your help to think through it in a way that honors you and is obedient to your Word." He always does.

Lie #4: "God Doesn't Care."
"I know God is powerful and can do anything. And I know he knows everything. So if he knows it all and can do it all, then the only reason he doesn't must be because he doesn't care."

The lie that God doesn't care is often at the root of other lies I believe. He doesn't truly care about my trials and problems in life. He doesn't care that this sickness is hard for me, or that this relationship crushes me. But this is a lie. In fact, it's the big lie underneath all the other lies we talked about.

At the very core of my soul, I've discovered I have a constant doubt about God's love for me. It's always creeping up to strangle the truth about God in my heart. I say "creeping" because it's so quiet, sneaky, and constant that I never seem to realize it's presence until I see the result: wicked weeds half-grown and choking out my faith in God's good character.

Every time I stop taking my problems to God, I can be sure of one thing: I've stopped believing in God's love. Oh sure, I might believe he loves me with a general, worldwide love, but not with a nitty-gritty, get-in-the-details love. How could he truly love me and allow these hard things into my life? After all, I wouldn't treat my beloved child the way God seems to be treating me. I try to shield my kids from the hurt and the hard. God must not love me as deeply as I love my children. So why should I bring my hurts to him when he's the one who gave them to me?

I know it sounds horribly raw (and maybe a little too honest?) when it's all written out like this in black and white. But do you see a reflection of your thoughts in this? Do you struggle to believe in God's love and care for you?

Sometimes I remind myself of a small child fighting against her mother. She needs that maternal comfort and love, but she won't be still long enough to receive it. Maybe she's even fighting against it because of something her mother did that she feels to be unkind. But when she allows herself to be loved by her mother and melt into her embrace, she finds a comfort far beyond her previous experiences.

When I fight against God by doubting his character—the fact that he loves me beyond my understanding—I make it impossible to rest in him and experience his love for me. I can't enjoy his good, unchanging love because I don't even believe it exists.

Dear friend, rest is found only when we go to the perfect lover of our souls to receive it. If we never run to him, how can we know his comfort? If we never take our hurts to him, how can we be healed? If we refuse to take the hard and heavy to his strong and capable hands, how can we know that his yoke is easy and his burden light? "Come unto me," Jesus calls. "Come, all you who are weary and heavily weighed down with cares, and you will find rest for your souls."

Maybe the reason you're worn out is because you're not going to the one who gives you rest. The only one who can give rest. He is the one who loves with a love that never gets tired or runs out. His is not a fake love that says "Let me know if you need anything!" but never delivers. It's a specific, personal love that sees deep inside my heart, knows all about me because he created me, understands my needs (whether surface or deep), and is able and willing to meet my every need.

We must come to him. Just like the fighting child doesn't enjoy the comfort of her mother's embrace, so I will never receive the comfort God wants to give me, as long as I push him away by insisting that "He doesn't truly love me."

Are you struggling to believe God's love? Come to him. Tell him. Rest in him.

"As the Father has loved me, so have I loved you. Abide in my love" (John 15:9).

He loves you. Believe him.

TWO FINAL
GROUND RULES

Remember Who You Are

Who are you? You are God's creation. Ruined by the curse, you are a sinner. If you believe in the person and work of Jesus Christ, you are a new creation and have become a child of God. "Therefore, if anyone is in Christ, he is a new creation. The old has passed away; behold, the new has come" (2 Corinthians 5:17).

Whether or not you believe in Christ, you belong to him. He has designed your life to function correctly only when you are surrendered to him, rather than fighting his work in your heart.

In short, you are a person who desperately needs Jesus. You need him because he made you, knows you, and gave his life for you. He has a claim on your heart.

Christa Threlfall

Remember Who He Is

Who is God? For starters, let's take a look at this story Jesus told in Luke 15.

"There was a man who had two sons. And the younger of them said to his father, 'Father, give me the share of property that is coming to me.' And he divided his property between them.

Not many days later, the younger son gathered all he had and took a journey into a far country, and there he squandered his property in reckless living. And when he had spent everything, a severe famine arose in that country, and he began to be in need. So he went and hired himself out to one of the citizens of that country, who sent him into his fields to feed pigs. And he was longing to be fed with the pods that the pigs ate, and no one gave him anything.

But when he came to himself, he said, 'How many of my father's hired servants have more than enough bread, but I perish here with hunger! I will arise and go to my father, and I will say to him, "Father, I have sinned against heaven and before you. I am no longer worthy to be called your son. Treat me as one of your hired servants."'

And he arose and came to his father. But while he was still a long way off, his father saw him and felt compassion, and ran and embraced him and kissed him. And the son said to him, 'Father, I have sinned against heaven and before you. I am no longer worthy to be called your son.'

But the father said to his servants, 'Bring quickly the best robe, and put it on him, and put a ring on his hand, and shoes on his feet. And bring the fattened calf and kill it, and let us eat and celebrate. For this my son was dead, and is alive again; he was lost, and is found.' And they began to celebrate."

This story portrays sinners as the two sons and God as the father. Remember: Jesus is the one who told this story. It isn't a clever illustration I made up, but a real metaphor for God and us, told by Christ himself. What does this story teach us about God?

He is compassionate.

"While he was still a long way off, his father saw him and felt compassion."

Was his father looking for him the whole time the son was gone? Or did he just happen to glance up and see the son returning? The passage doesn't tell us, but it does say that as soon as the father saw his son returning, his response was one not of judgment or condemnation, but of compassion.

Compassion! After what his son did? Taking his money, refusing to help on the family farm, wasting his father's inheritance, and then returning with nothing to show but an apology?

Yes. He responds with compassion. Do you view God this way? Remember that he is compassionate—not just to the masses, but to you.

He meets us where we are.

"His father saw him and felt compassion, and ran."

This father wasn't afraid of appearing "too eager" for this boy of his who had just disgraced the family name. He didn't stand stoically at the end of the driveway to see what his son had to say for himself. As soon as the father saw his boy coming home, he ran to him!

We often have this idea of God as a Father who is looking down on us in displeasure. And if we fail him? Well, there's

Christa Threlfall

no hope for us. But this is not the way God describes himself! Remember that God meets you with compassion.

He publicly shows affection for us.
"and ran and embraced him and kissed him."

Jesus says the father welcomes his son with hugs and kisses. That in itself is amazing, considering the history this father and son have experienced together. But notice the timing. The father has not yet heard his son's apology when he embraces him! He doesn't know why his son is returning, only that he's finally come home. And with that bit of knowledge, he responds by expressing public affection for his son.

What does this teach us about God? God loves me because I am his. Not because I offered an apology. Not because I told him I would be his servant. But because he is my Father. And that is enough.

He loves us extravagantly.
"And the son said to him, 'Father, I have sinned against heaven and before you. I am no longer worthy to be called your son.' But the father said to his servants, 'Bring quickly the best robe, and put it on him, and put a ring on his hand, and shoes on his feet.'"

After the way this son disgraced the family name and refused to help at his father's estate, it would have been loving for the father to hire his son as one of his servants. But he goes far beyond that. Instead, he listens to his son's apology and comes back with a different option. I love how the story puts it: "but the father said." But. His son says, "I have sinned and I'm not worth to even be called your son." But the father says, "Yeah, I hear you. But I've got something else in mind, son." Then he turns to his servants (the very ranks of which the son wanted to join) and commands them to bring out the very best robe, ring, and sandals for his boy. He welcomes him back not as a servant, but as his son with an extravagant display of love.

Do you view God this way? Remember that he responds to your apology, not just with acceptance, but with an extravagant display of love for you.

He celebrates when we return.

"And bring the fattened calf and kill it, and let us eat and celebrate. For this my son was dead, and is alive again; he was lost, and is found.' And they began to celebrate."

"Alright, fine. Come in the house and tell me what you did with all my money," the father growls. "Tell me how it is that you left in fine clothes and returned in rags."

Perhaps we imagine God responds this way when we come to him. We view him as an angry dad, impossible to please. But when Jesus tells this story, he says the father's response is not to stiff-arm his son, but to celebrate him.

Do you believe this? Do you believe that God celebrates when you come to him? Jesus said it first! So often we have the idea that when we return to God, we have to sit in a time-out chair for a little while. Or maybe we have to be long-faced and sorrowful for a few weeks. But that's not what this father did. He listened to his son's apology, then threw out commands to his servants. Not commands to take the son and throw him into the servant's quarters. Instead, he threw a party! His child had come home! This is cause for celebration!

My friend, this story is a mirror of God's actions towards us. To come to Jesus, we must remember the true character of God. Discard the lies in your heart and listen instead to Jesus' words about himself. Your Heavenly Father is compassionate. He meets you where you are. He shows affection and showers extravagant love on you. And he celebrates when you come to him. *This* is our God. Who wouldn't want to come to a God like this?

Conclusion

It's sobering to think how easily I can hear truth but refuse to let it change me. In fact, I've discovered that sometimes I hear truth so frequently and become so accustomed to it that I begin to believe I obey it even though my actions remain the same.

These words of God regularly pierce my heart: "Be doers of the word, and not hearers only, deceiving yourselves. For if anyone is a hearer of the word and not a doer, he is like a man who looks intently at his natural face in a mirror. For he looks at himself and goes away and at once forgets what he was like. But the one who looks into the perfect law, the law of liberty, and perseveres, being no hearer who forgets but a doer who acts, he will be blessed in his doing" (James 1:22-25).

Our hearts are notoriously capable of self-deception. You can read this book and agree with the message—even become convicted by God's Spirit—yet refuse to actually change. I can write this book and encourage you to come to Jesus, yet refuse to take my struggles to him. Exposing our hearts to truth is only profitable when we allow that truth to change us.

You have read truth in these pages. God wants you to come to him with everything. But your heart and habits can only be changed as you submit your will to God's and run to him with your struggles.

What if God designs your days to keep you running back to him? *He does.*

Will you come to Jesus today?
There is no better place to rest.

About the Author

Christa Threlfall grew up in a pastor's home as the youngest of four siblings. She trusted Jesus as her Savior when she was a young girl and had the opportunity to serve in various church ministries, both in the United States and abroad. After graduating with her B.S. in Elementary Education, she married Jonathan and their family expanded from two to six. They currently reside in New Hampshire where Christa serves as a pastor's wife. She enjoys exploring with her kids, laughing and eating ice cream with Jonathan, being active outdoors, and spending time with her church family. You can find more of her writings at BrownSugarToast.com.